Essential Viewpoints

GENETIC
ENGINEERING

Essential Viewpoints

GENETIC
ENGINEERING

BY THOMAS PARMALEE

Content Consultant
Josephine Johnston LL.B., MBHL, Associate for Law and Bioethics
Director of Research Operations, The Hastings Center
Garrison, New York

ABDO
Publishing Company

CREDITS

Published by ABDO Publishing Company, 8000 West 78th Street, Edina, Minnesota 55439. Copyright © 2008 by Abdo Consulting Group, Inc. International copyrights reserved in all countries. No part of this book may be reproduced in any form without written permission from the publisher. The Essential Library™ is a trademark and logo of ABDO Publishing Company.

Printed in the United States.

Editor: Jill Sherman
Copy Editor: Paula Lewis
Interior Design and Production: Rebecca Daum
Cover Design: Rebecca Daum

Library of Congress Cataloging-in-Publication Data
Parmalee, Thomas.
  Genetic engineering / Thomas Parmalee.
    p. cm. — (Essential viewpoints)
  Includes bibliographical references and index.
  ISBN 978-1-60453-057-5
  1. Genetic engineering—Juvenile literature. 2. Genetic engineering—Social aspects—Juvenile literature. 3. Medical genetics—Juvenile literature. I. Title.

  QH442.P373 2008
  174'.957—dc22

                              2007031917

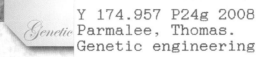

TABLE OF CONTENTS

Dolly was cloned in 1996.

GENETIC ENGINEERING:
ITS HIGHS AND LOWS

*I*magine being able to cure fatal diseases by
eliminating defective genes, make crops
that are resistant to pests, or end genetic disorders
such as sickle-cell anemia or even some forms of
cancer. Some scientists believe all of this will one day

be possible through genetic engineering. But others wonder if it is ethical to tamper with genes.

Genetic engineering is a complex science. Genetic refers to genes. A gene is part of DNA (*deoxyribonucleic acid*). It carries chemical information that gives people and other living things many of their personal characteristics or traits. The color of a person's eyes and the type of fur a dog has are controlled by genes. However, many traits are determined by a combination of genes and the environment. Engineering refers to creation. Most people are familiar with the idea of engineering bridges and other structures. Genetic scientists have taken the idea of engineering a step further by trying to change (or in some cases create new) living organisms such as bacteria, plants, animals, and human beings.

Genetic engineering is any scientific method of controlling the genetic makeup of an organism. Scientists are testing new ways to control the traits of an organism so that, for example, it looks a certain way or produces a certain chemical.

Who Coined the Term "Genetic Engineering?"

Genetic engineering is a fairly recent term. Danish microbiologist A. Jost first used the term while he was giving a lecture regarding the sex life of yeast at the Technical Institute in Lwow, Poland, in 1941.

The Heart of the Controversy

People disagree about whether genetic engineering does more harm than good and whether it is moral or immoral. Some scientists believe that genetic engineering could be used to cure a number of diseases. They think that it could even be used to prolong life and give people super-human traits. Some scientists argue that planting genetically modified crops that are resistant to pesticides helps the environment and could help end world hunger.

But there are those who fear that genetic engineering could be used for

Dolly the Sheep

Dolly was born on July 5, 1996, but was not announced to the public until February 1997. She was cloned at the Roslin Institute in Edinburgh, Scotland, by a team managed by Ian Wilmut.

Dolly was the first mammal successfully cloned from a specialized adult cell. Dolly was cloned from another sheep's mammary cell. Wilmut's team had already cloned two sheep from embryonic cells before Dolly. Embryonic cells can develop into any other specialized cells, so they are easier to use in cloning. What made Dolly special was that she was cloned from an existing adult sheep, using a specialized cell. Specialized cells are more difficult to use in cloning because they are not as versatile in their development as embryonic cells.

Dolly's birth sparked a fiery debate about cloning. Some saw her birth as a great scientific success. Others worried that science had gone too far and felt that cloning was unethical.

Dolly died in 2003 at the age of six. This is shorter than the average life span of a sheep. It cannot be determined whether cloning played a role in her death. For some people, Dolly's early death renewed the debate over cloning.

terrorism, war, or to separate classes of people. Some object to genetic engineering on religious grounds. They argue that God, not humans, should be in the business of either creating or modifying living things. Others say that pests that harm crops will become resistant to the new crops, and those pests will become more difficult to control.

In 2003, the public's interest in human genetic engineering was on the forefront. That year, scientists announced they had successfully mapped the human genome. A genome is the full DNA sequence in an organism. This map could open the door to further study into human genes.

THE HUMAN GENOME PROJECT

The Human Genome Project was a massive undertaking. It began in 1990 and was scheduled to last 15 years. The project was finished two years early because of advances in technology.

The goals of the Human Genome Project were to:

❖ Identify all the genes in human DNA.

❖ Store the information gathered.

❖ Improve data analysis of the information.

❖ Transfer technologies for use in industries.

❖ Address legal, ethical, and social issues that may develop as a result of the project.

The Human Genome Project was important for many reasons. It brought attention to genetic engineering, and it helped fuel the biotechnology industry, which has become an important part of the world economy. The project also served to address some of the ethical questions that have made genetic engineering so controversial.

After mapping out the human genome, some scientists believed that it would only be a short time before science could find a cure for cancer and other diseases. Such cures have yet to emerge, but there has been progress in researching treatments. Many of these treatments were developed from genetic engineering research.

The cost of researching the genomes of living organisms has decreased. In 1990, it cost ten dollars to sequence each base pair. By 2005, the cost was only one-tenth of one cent. As a result, more scientists were able to decode the genomes of organisms. Scientists may be able to use that information and apply it to current research.

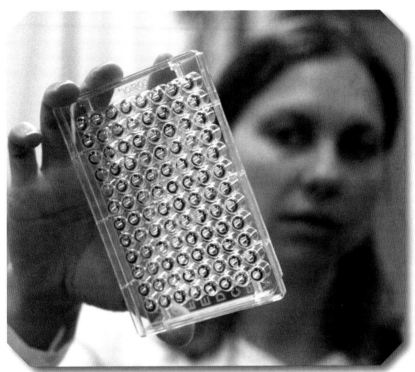

This tray of human DNA is undergoing sequencing to map the human genome.

In Favor: Genetic Engineering Successes

Genetic engineering is already used on a wide scale in agriculture. For instance, chymosin, an enzyme that is used to make cheese, is often produced using genetic engineering. The traditional method of making the enzyme is not as efficient as genetic engineering. In addition, many genetically engineered crops are resistant to disease and insect infestation. There are even foods that are entirely genetically engineered.

Genetic engineering has also been used to treat some diseases. In September 2006, Steven Rosenburg, chief of surgery at the U.S. National Cancer Institute in Bethesda, Maryland, reported that they had successfully cured two men with terminal cases of cancer by using genetic engineering. Both men had been given six months to live but were saved by the treatment based on genetic engineering.

However, while there are examples of genetic engineering being used to cure fatal diseases, it does not work in all cases. The results are inconsistent and there is much to learn. Also, most treatments are being performed only on patients who are already near death. The government

Flavr-Savr Tomato

The Flavr-Savr tomato was the first genetically engineered food to be licensed for human consumption. The tomato was produced by a company called Calgene in California. The tomato was submitted to the Food and Drug Administration (FDA) in 1992. The FDA determined that labeling these tomatoes as genetically modified was unnecessary because there was no evidence of health risks and the nutritional content of the tomatoes was the same as of tomatoes that were not modified.

requires that treatments undergo testing to show that they are safe and effective before these treatments are available to the general public.

Genetic engineering has also been used to fight diabetes, a disease that affects millions of people. In the two types of diabetes, the person's body either does not produce insulin or is not able to use it well. Diabetes can damage a person's kidneys and eyes and cause heart disease. Insulin was the first commercial product that was the result of genetic engineering. It was brought to the market in the early 1980s. In genetically engineered insulin, bacteria and yeast are modified by adding the human gene sequence for insulin production. The bacteria and yeast can then produce the insulin that diabetics need to survive.

OPPOSED: GENETIC ENGINEERING FAILURES

The dangers of genetic engineering made headlines after 18-year-old Jesse Gelsinger died on September 17, 1999, as a result of his participation in a medical

Genetic Diseases

Genetic diseases (or genetic disorders) are caused by abnormal genes or chromosomes. Some genetic diseases are acquired during life, but most are either present at conception or are inherited. These include Down syndrome, Huntington's disease, cystic fibrosis, sickle-cell anemia, and others. Most diseases, however, result from a combination of genetics and the environment.

trial. Medical trials test a certain medical treatment to see if it is safe, effective, and ready for the public. Although he was not sick at the time of the study, Gelsinger suffered from a potentially fatal genetic disease and had been participating in a genetic engineering, or gene therapy, trial at the University of Pennsylvania. Gelsinger and the other patients in the trial were treated for a deficiency of an enzyme that the liver uses to break down ammonia.

Scientists engineered a virus that would transfer genetic information to the patient's cells. In genetic engineering, viruses are often used for this purpose. However, in Gelsinger's case, the virus triggered a series of events that led to his death.

The news that genetic engineering had caused a teenager's death spread across the United States. It was the first death directly attributed to genetic engineering. Gelsinger's death became the most widely publicized genetic engineering failure up to that date.

An investigation by the FDA revealed that the scientists involved could not prove that all of their subjects met the criteria for the study. Also, the consent form did not inform the subjects that monkeys had died from a similar treatment. The institute was forced to temporarily stop all gene-therapy trials.

In another case, the company Avigen stopped a trial in 2004 that sought to treat hemophilia patients. Hemophilia is an inherited disease in which the person's blood does not clot. After a cut or a bruise, the body may bleed internally or externally. This rare disease is painful and can be life threatening. Avigen chose to stop the trial after two of seven patients developed elevated levels of liver enzymes. Trials are often stopped if such complications occur.

Mixed Results

Genetic engineering experiments are rarely complete successes or failures. For instance, one study began in March 1999 to treat children with Severe Combined Immunodeficiency (SCID). Children with SCID lack

Biomachines

It may sound like science fiction, but Dr. Drew Endy, a professor at MIT, foresees a day in which micro machines will travel throughout human bodies and hunt down cancer cells and other dangerous entities. These custom-crafted biomachines could prevent disease, kill old cells, or create new fuels.

In 2005, Endy and three partners started the Codon Devices company in Cambridge, Massachusetts. Codon Devices received $13 million in funding to sell genetic material to companies that seek to make such micro machines. Eventually, the firm wants to create its own micro machines to be used in the body.

T-lymphocytes, a type of immune cell. SCID is fatal within one year.

Ten children took part in the trial. Three of the children developed a disease similar to leukemia, which caused an uncontrolled production of T-lymphocytes. Two of those children were successfully treated, but one of them died. Nine of the ten children were effectively cured of SCID, a fatal disease. But it was not easy.

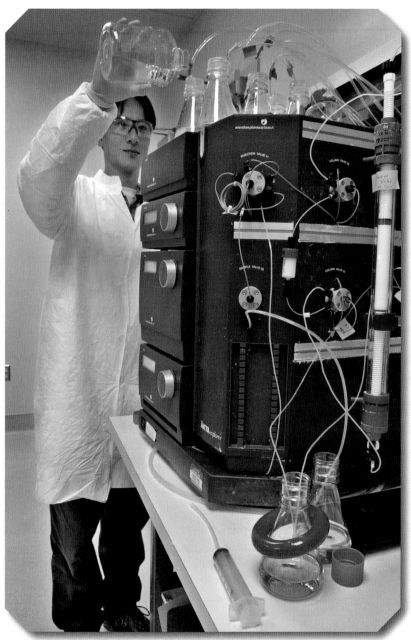

A researcher at Avigen is pursuing gene-therapy treatments.

Genetic engineering involves the manipulation of DNA.

WHAT IS GENETIC ENGINEERING?

An organism's traits are, in part, determined by its DNA, which is the organism's genetic material. DNA carries the instructions for building, maintaining, and reproducing cells.

Sections of DNA called genes each control one trait by controlling how proteins are made. Proteins are important because they make up cells. Some proteins make up the cell's structure. Other proteins are enzymes and catalysts. These proteins control chemical reactions in a cell. These reactions affect the way a cell grows and develops. Genes contribute to things such as a person's hair color and height. They also affect whether a person will develop some diseases such as sickle-cell anemia.

Genetic engineers replace genes with those of another organism or alter existing genes. By doing this, new proteins are made and an organism's traits can be changed.

Moving genes from one organism to another is not a new idea. It has been done for thousands of years. When farmers selected animals that were larger and healthier to breed 10,000 years ago, they were hoping that the offspring of those animals would inherit the beneficial traits of the animals' parents.

Farmers have selectively paired crops for thousands of years as well. When a farmer pollinates one plant with another, he or she is manipulating the genes of the offspring.

One scientist who made great progress in discovering how traits are passed on was Gregor Mendel. Mendel is often called "the father of genetics." He experimented on pea plants from 1856 to 1863. Through his experiments, Mendel was able to purify a desired trait in a pea plant through self-pollination. He then bred the offspring that contained the desired trait with a plant that had a different trait. By studying the results of his experiments, he formulated a theory about recessive and dominant traits. Dominant traits overshadow recessive traits. Recessive traits are evident in offspring only if each parent has passed down the recessive gene.

Watson and Crick

Scientists could never have really pursued the ideas behind genetic engineering without determining the structure of deoxyribonucleic acid, or DNA. Francis Crick and James Watson made that discovery in 1953. At about that same time, Rosalind Franklin and Maurice Wilkins made similar findings.

Watson and Crick showed that DNA consists of a double helix and that it carries the genetic information that is the key to hereditary traits. The two DNA strands that form the double helix consist of four nucleotide bases—adenine, thymine, cytosine, and guanine. Adenine always pairs with thymine. Cytosine always pairs with guanine. This discovery showed that by knowing the sequence of nucleotides on one strand of DNA, the sequence on the other strand can be determined. The two scientists announced their discovery on April 25, 1953, in a letter to *Nature* magazine.

Watson, Crick, and Wilkins were awarded the Nobel Prize in Physiology or Medicine in 1962 for unraveling the mystery of DNA.

SELECTIVE BREEDING

Early experiments with genetics, however, are not usually thought of as genetic engineering. Instead, this is called selective breeding, which describes a transfer of genes that would not occur in nature. One of the main differences between selective breeding and genetic engineering is that selective breeding usually involves two species that are closely related. Genetic engineering, on the other hand, may involve combining the genes of two very different species. In addition, selective breeding uses natural biological processes to help create new types of crops and livestock.

When people began farming land approximately 10,000 years ago, they selected wild grasses for selective breeding. These wild grasses led to the cultivation of crops such as wheat, rice, and maize (corn). Farmers proceeded to replant only seeds that came from particular plants because those plants produced the best product during harvest. By doing this, farmers were engaging in a practice that

Gregor Mendel

Years after Mendel's experiments took place, an abbot at the Czech Republic monastery where Mendel had lived burned many of the records Mendel had kept. As a result, it is difficult to know exactly whether Mendel understood the full importance of his experiments. People did not understand what genes were during his lifetime.

changed the environment to suit their purposes.

Farmers also manipulated food by using microorganisms such as bacteria and yeast in the fermentation of beer and in the production of yogurt. Early on, farmers were familiar with hybrids, which were new types of plants produced by crossbreeding related varieties of plants.

Selective breeding had an effect on animals as well. A male donkey was first bred with a female horse to create a mule more than 3,000 years ago. Mules were first used to transport items, and are still used today to carry goods.

Breeding Traits

A retired male racehorse can still be sold for a large amount of money because the horse can be bred with a mare. Breeders hope that the offspring of that fast horse will share some of the traits of its parents. Unfortunately, genes alone do not determine most traits and the chance of a horse passing on its speed is not very likely. One famous racehorse, Seabiscuit, fathered more than 100 foals. Only a few of his offspring were successful in races.

DIFFERENCES IN SELECTIVE BREEDING AND GENETIC ENGINEERING

There are three main differences between selective breeding and genetic engineering. First, selective breeding involves breeding within a species or the crossing of species that are closely related. Second, the pace of change in selective breeding is slower compared to genetic engineering. Selective breeding requires traits to be developed over several generations, whereas a genetic engineer can insert a gene from one organism into another organism in a matter of days. Third, selective breeding only modifies a small number of species. Genetic engineering, however, can change a whole variety of organisms for a variety of purposes. Some of the areas in which genetic engineering seeks to produce change are sewage disposal, pollution control, and drug production.

The difference between genetic engineering and selective breeding can be confusing because the two fields are closely related. However, genetic engineering involves advanced scientific processes. The science behind genetic engineering is highly sophisticated and advances in the technology are being made every day.

Charles Darwin

Charles Robert Darwin is most remembered for his book of theories on evolution, *On the Origin of Species by Means of Natural Selection*, published in 1859.

During his travels throughout South America and the Galapagos Islands in the Pacific Ocean, Darwin noticed variations among closely related plants and animals. Darwin theorized that over millions of years, animals with beneficial genetic traits were able to survive longer than their peers. He called this process natural selection.

How Does Genetic Engineering Work?

Genetic engineering methods are not simple, and they constantly change with the development of new technologies. But the basic premise remains the same: Scientists combine the genes of one organism with the genes of another or otherwise modify a gene. There are three methods scientists typically use: the plasmid method, the vector method, and the biolistic method. However, other methods or variations of these methods are also being used.

The plasmid method is the most widely used method by scientists to alter genes. Using this method, scientists can remove a section of DNA from one organism and replace it with the DNA of another organism. This modified DNA is then allowed to absorb into bacteria, which incorporate the DNA into their own structure. The bacteria with the new DNA are then allowed to divide and pass along the new genetic material.

Genzyme Genetics

Scientists can do genetic testing on human embryos during assisted reproduction to determine whether a baby will be healthy. One company that does these tests is Genzyme Genetics. This company is a worldwide provider of diagnostic testing and genetic counseling services. Genetic counselors at Genzyme determine what diseases or disorders a baby might develop if a specific embryo was to be implanted into a woman. They also answer questions that potential parents might have about their embryo.

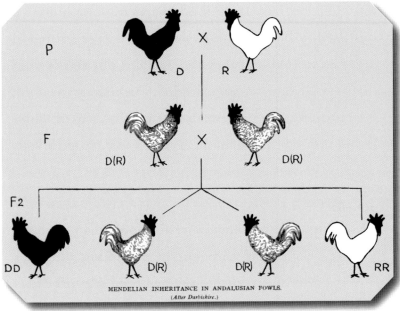

P

X

D | R

F

X

D(R) | D(R)

F2

DD | D(R) | D(R) | RR

MENDELIAN INHERITANCE IN ANDALUSIAN FOWLS.
(After Darbishire.)

Some traits are inherited from parental genes.

The vector method is similar to the plasmid method. After scientists have created a new strand of DNA, it is directly inserted into known genomes using a virus. Viruses insert their DNA into healthy cells. The cells then reproduce with the virus's DNA. This is how viruses reproduce.

To use viruses for genetic engineering, large portions of a virus's DNA must be removed. If this were not done, the virus would still be harmful. New DNA can then be inserted into the virus, which will insert the new DNA into the genome being modified.

The biolistic method is often used when genetic engineers seek to modify the DNA in plants. In this method, metal pellets are coated with modified DNA and are fired at plant cells. Some of the cells take up the new DNA. Scientists allow these cells to grow.

Cloning

Another form of genetic engineering is cloning. In cloning, genetic information is copied from a single organism. To do this, scientists remove or inactivate the nucleus of an egg cell, or oocyte. The nucleus contains a cell's genetic information. Scientists can then introduce the nuclear material from another cell. The oocyte will then grow into a cloned embryo.

Scientists can clone individual cells or an entire organism. A clone has genetic material almost identical to that of the donor organism. Scientists use cloning to replicate desirable traits.

Mules are the result of crossbreeding.

A researcher removes plasmid DNA for research.

ARGUMENTS FOR
GENETIC ENGINEERING

*D*espite the concerns that many people have about genetic engineering, there are also many scientists and members of the general public who believe that genetic engineering serves many important purposes.

In Favor: Growing Genetically Modified Foods Could Help the Environment

Advocates of agricultural genetic engineering argue that the technology allows farmers to grow a greater amount of crops on the same amount of land. As a result, less land is used. That unused land can then be preserved. Moreover, many argue that genetic engineering could be used to feed the hungry.

In addition, genetically engineered crops that are resistant to pests will help the environment. Farmers would not have to spray their crops with pesticides, which are harmful to a variety of living things and can pollute the water supply.

Scientists also hope to genetically engineer crops that could clean pollutants from soil, sediment, and water sources.

Ahead of Their Time

In 1972, Theodore Friedmann and Richard Roblin published the first detailed paper on the possibility of treating genetic diseases by transferring genes from one organism to another. "Gene Therapy for Human Genetic Disease?" was published in *Science* magazine. Although they were aware of the potential benefits of genetic engineering, the scientists also were the first to mention the ethical concerns and potential risks that genetic engineering presented.

Scientists also hope to be able to modify plants so they can remove heavy metals from polluted soil. Such plants could possibly store toxic substances in their cells, thereby removing the toxins from the ground.

Another possible benefit to genetic engineering would be the ability to make foods healthier or to remove allergens in certain foods that prevent everyone from enjoying them. Scientists working on genetically modified foods say that they are safe. Clive James is the director of the International Service for the Acquisition of Agri-Biotech Applications, a nonprofit group that promotes biotechnology. According to James, "Three hundred million people in the U.S. and Canada have been eating (genetically modified foods) for 10 years with not even a hint of a problem."[1]

A Better Mosquito

Malaria infects between 300 and 500 million people per year and kills as many as 1 million people. But scientists have engineered a type of mosquito that cannot transmit the disease. Although mosquitoes with malaria can live, their ability to breed is affected. It is believed that genetically engineered mosquitoes that cannot transmit malaria would outcompete their natural counterparts.

In Favor: Genetic Engineering Could Revolutionize Medicine

Scientists believe there are many ways that genetic engineering could improve the quality of life. Genetic engineering is used to produce insulin, which diabetics rely on to live a normal life. There is hope that, in the future, genetic engineering could be used so that diabetics would not have to take injected insulin at all—or at least not as often.

Moreover, genetic engineering has been used to treat some forms of cancer and other deadly diseases. Such treatments are not always successful, but many scientists argue that over time, techniques will be perfected.

Researchers are trying to use genetic engineering methods to grow new organs.

Treatment for Male Infertility

In April 2007, German scientists reported they had successfully created early versions of sperm cells from bone marrow. Professor Karim Nayernia, then working at the University of Gottingen, led the research project. Nayernia's team isolated stem cells extracted from bone marrow donated by male volunteers. Scientists stimulated the stem cells with a form of vitamin A so that the stem cells would become male reproductive cells.

Analysis of the cells showed that they contained "spermatagonial stem cells," which are an early version of male sperm cells. Though the cells cannot yet be transformed into sperm cells, researchers hope to find a way to manipulate the cells to do so. They hope that their work will one day help infertile couples.

These organs could be used for people who need transplants. One way this could be done is by transferring human DNA into a human egg cell, which then could be grown into virtually any kind of cell.

Scientists also hope to develop organs for transplant that humans can better tolerate. In 2002, Alan Flake of the Children's Hospital in Philadelphia and Esmail Zanjani of the University of Nevada placed human stem cells into sheep fetuses. When the lambs were born, their tissues, including blood, cartilage, muscle, and their hearts, displayed human characteristics of almost 40 percent. The external body features were always animal-like, but the genetic makeup made it much more likely that their organs would have had a chance of being tolerated

Alteration of Salmon

Elliot Entis, owner of Aqua Bounty Technologies, has been trying to introduce a fast-growing type of salmon to the marketplace for years. Upon approval from the FDA, the company plans to release the salmon in 2008.

The salmon produced by Aqua Bounty grow quickly because the salmon's DNA contains a specific gene that causes them to grow year-round. In normal salmon, this gene is only activated by the strong sunlight of spring and summer. The salmon could cut costs for fish farmers by 35 percent and allow the farmers to double their output. There would be no difference in taste between the normal salmon and the genetically altered salmon.

Researchers modify viruses to be used for gene therapy.

in a human. Scientists have conducted similar experiments with pigs and other animals.

In Favor: Opportunities for Other Uses Abound

Some believe genetic engineering could one day be used to make people better—as in smarter, healthier, and even better looking. Though it is uncertain whether these traits can be genetically engineered, researchers are exploring the possibility.

Many hope that genetic engineering could one day be used to cure people of genetic diseases. Likewise, genetic testing of embryos would allow parents to choose to implant an embryo into a woman's uterus only if it were free of any genetic defects. These steps would help ensure good health.

Advocates of genetic engineering also point out the possibility that cloning could be used to produce embryonic stem cells that could then be matched with individual patients who need particular tissues or organs.

Cloning also has the potential to reproduce elite livestock. This could help reduce the risk of livestock developing genetic diseases and produce higher quality products.

Genetically modified barley

Catholic Archbishop Raymond Burke speaks out against stem cell research and cloning.

ARGUMENTS AGAINST
GENETIC ENGINEERING

ome opponents of genetic engineering
object to it because they believe it violates
the natural order. Some object based on religious
grounds, arguing that God alone is responsible for
creating and modifying living things. Others argue

that the lasting effects are unknown and that it is simply too dangerous.

Opposed: Genetic Engineering Is Dangerous

In 1998 and 1999, while trying to create a virus that would sterilize mice, scientists at the Australian National University in Canberra accidentally created a virus that crippled the mice's immune systems and killed them. The experiment did not cause much controversy at that time. However, the gene contained in mice that paralyzed their immune systems is also found in humans. There was concern that the same virus that killed the mice could possibly kill humans.

Steven M. Block, a Stanford biologist, is concerned about creating strange new viruses. He expressed his concern about viruses getting into the wrong hands, saying, "We're tempted to say that nobody in their right mind would ever use these things. But not everybody is in their right mind."[1]

Opposed: Genetic Engineering Is Expensive

Another drawback to genetic engineering is that it tends to be expensive. In recent years, Congress and members of the public have worked to find ways to cut the price of health care. Drugs made by biotechnology companies can cost tens of thousands of dollars a year per patient. The cost of drugs produced by biotechnology companies reached $40 billion in 2005. While many of these drugs help treat a variety of diseases and illnesses, critics say the price is too high.

Critics also point out that genetic engineering poses a problem of access. Who will be able to use these technologies and take advantage of them? In many cases, costly new technologies will not be affordable to everyone. For instance, one day it may be possible for couples to have certain genes implanted into the embryos of their children that would give the children an advantage. This procedure would

Some Go to Extremes

Some opponents of genetic engineering go too far. Authorities believe a group of radical environmentalists set fire to a research laboratory at the University of Washington Center for Urban Horticulture in May 2001. The blaze destroyed two buildings and several vehicles. A fire set at the same time destroyed a nearby tree nursery.

Police believe the lab was targeted because it conducted research involving genetically modified foods. The tree farm was affiliated with a university group that conducted genetic engineering experiments.

Radical groups opposed to genetic engineering sometimes go to extremes in their protests. Most individuals against genetic engineering, however, do not condone such actions.

only be available to those who could afford it.

Opposed: Unknown Effects

Jeremy Rifkin is an economist and author who founded the Foundation of Economic Trends in Washington, D.C. He has also lectured at more than 300 universities, expressing serious concern about the effects of genetic engineering. Rifkin fears that genetic engineering could be dangerous. He asks:

> *Will the creation of cloned ... species mean the end of nature? Will the mass release of genetically engineered organisms into our biosphere mean genetic pollution and irreversible damage to the biosphere in the twenty-first century? What are the risks of making a 'perfect' baby?*[2]

Rifkin points out that while humans have been crossbreeding

Opponents of Genetic Engineering Gather Online

Europeans tend to take a harder line against genetic engineering than do U.S. citizens. Many Europeans gather online to exchange ideas and to oppose genetic engineering. One such Web site that caters to opponents of genetic modification (GM) in the United Kingdom is the Genetic Engineering Network. This group opposes GM food, human and animal genetic engineering, and biotechnology companies. This network "helps to facilitate exchange between individuals and groups within the British anti-GM campaign."[3]

Groups that exchange information on the network include Corporate Watch, Earth First!, Genetix Food Alert, Five Year Freeze, Green Party, Greenpeace, Women's Environmental Network, and Gaia Foundation, as well as natural food stores, organic farmers, and other groups and individuals.

different organisms for centuries, the resulting organisms have never been able to reproduce. By releasing genetically engineered species into the wild, scientists will lose control over how the species reproduce. Any mistakes will be difficult, if not impossible, to correct.

Opposed: Eliminated Genes May Be Important

There are other even more serious drawbacks to genetic engineering. According to Rifkin, as scientists select traits they believe to be superior, they will reduce the gene pool and kill off other traits whose importance scientists may not fully understand. Rifkin worries about what will happen to society if certain genes begin to die out. Rifkin goes so far as to predict that wealthy individuals could become genetically superior.

Opposition to Human Cloning

In many opinion polls, large numbers of respondents have said that they do not support human cloning. Religious people are slightly more prone to object to the practice. An analysis of a 2001 ABC poll showed that 95 percent of evangelical Protestants wanted human cloning to be illegal, compared with 91 percent of Catholics, 83 percent of non-evangelical Protestants, and 77 percent of people who said they were not religious.

Protestors want genetically engineered food to be labeled.

"This commercial competition and conflict over ownership and control of the gene pool will further divide the haves and the have-nots," Rifkin said.[4]

Scientists who favor genetic engineering often argue that the market will decide its fate. This means that science will progress in areas in which people have interest and from which companies can make a profit. The idea infuriates Rifkin. "To me, the most chilling prospect of all is letting the marketplace and consumers decide the future evolution of our species and other creatures," he said.[5]

Greenpeace

One group against genetic engineering is Greenpeace, which aims to protect the environment. Greenpeace has waged a worldwide campaign against genetically modified organisms, particularly in food.

According to Greenpeace, "GMOs [genetically modified organisms] should not be released into the environment as there is not adequate scientific understanding of their impact on the environment and human health."[6] The organization has also sought to promote a ban on selling genetically modified foods.

OPPOSED: METHODS MAY NOT BE SAFE

Some opponents of genetic engineering fear that modified bacteria could come in contact with natural bacteria. The natural bacteria could then assume modified traits. They also fear that modified plants could pass on their genetic variations to wild plants. The concern is that this would have harmful effects on the environment and living things.

Opponents to genetic engineering also are concerned about the use of viruses in genetic engineering. They fear that the virus could interfere with cells in unintended ways. The danger involved could put people at risk.

A Greenpeace activist warns against allowing genetically engineered pharmaceutical crops to be grown outdoors.

Steven Druker of the Alliance for Bio-Integrity shows the many products that can include genetically engineered ingredients.

GENETICALLY MODIFIED FOOD

What if food tasted great but had fewer calories? What if peanut butter did not cause negative reactions in people with allergies? What if tropical fruit could be grown in the cold regions of the United States, which could then be sold in the supermarket at lower prices? Scientists believe that all of these things are possible through genetic engineering.

Regardless of whether or not they realize it, most people in the United States have probably already eaten genetically modified food. Cereal, soda, baked snacks, and cooking oil are just some of the products that regularly make use of genetic engineering. As of 2005, the amount of farmland used to grow genetically engineered crops was estimated at 222 million acres (90 million ha) worldwide. The United States is the world leader in growing genetically engineered food. It grows more than half of such crops. Twenty other countries also grow genetically modified food.

Soybeans, corn, cotton, and canola have been engineered to be resistant to particular insects or herbicides. Scientists are also trying

Solving World Hunger

Some people believe that producing more genetically modified food would solve world hunger. But according to Margaret Mellon, a director with the Union of Concerned Scientists, "We have sufficient food now, but it doesn't get to those who need it. Most hungry people simply can't afford to buy what's already out there even when commodity prices are at all-time lows. How does genetic engineering address the problem of income disparity?"[1]

Roger H. Salquist of Calgene displays two genetically altered tomatoes.

to create crops that would be more productive and resistant to drought and viruses.

The tomato, the first food developed by genetic engineering, was approved to be sold in the United States by the FDA in May 1994. The company that produced it, Calgene, called it the Flavr-Savr because scientists had taken out a gene that causes tomatoes to soften and reinserted it backward. The tomato was then able to stay on the vine longer. Theoretically, the Flavr-Savr had more flavor because naturally grown tomatoes need to be taken off the vine when they are still green and firm. Otherwise, they would be damaged during transport. But the Flavr-Savr could stay on the vine until it was red and ripe.

In December 2006, the worldwide market for commercial seeds was reported at about $25 billion, with the United States accounting for $5.7 billion of that total. Farmers were willing to pay for seeds that would be resistant to herbicides and disease. In 2005, 87 percent of the soybean crop in the United States consisted of herbicide-tolerant varieties, and 61 percent of the cotton crop consisted of such varieties.

OPPOSED: GENETICALLY MODIFIED CROPS MAY HARM THE ENVIRONMENT

People who oppose the genetic engineering of food have legitimate concerns. Although genetically

Genetically Modified Foods Are Unpopular in Europe

Most American supermarkets sell genetically modified foods, even though a person may not be aware of it. But in Europe, every major food distributor and supermarket has banned genetically modified food. Europeans and European governments are not accepting of genetically modified foods and will not buy them.

Some American supermarkets, however, have followed Europe's example. In December 1999, Whole Foods and Wild Oats, which sell natural foods, announced that they would not use genetically modified foods in their own product brands, and they discourage suppliers from doing so.

engineered food has been available for years, some find it disturbing that scientists cannot definitively say whether such crops have a harmful effect on the environment.

In 1999, researchers at Cornell University showed that monarch caterpillars that ate pollen from a type of genetically engineered corn died. The corn had been engineered to produce a toxin that is fatal to the European corn borer pest. Scientists did not realize the toxin was also fatal to monarch butterflies. An in-depth study on the toxin's effects would be costly. Also, because the monarch butterfly is not an endangered species, further study was deemed unnecessary.

OPPOSED: GENETICALLY MODIFIED PLANTS COULD SPREAD

Some people fear that genetically engineered crops could spread uncontrollably and have unforeseen effects on nature. For instance, insects may be able to carry pollen from a genetically engineered plant to an undesirable relative, such as an invasive weed. This weed could assume the characteristics of the genetically engineered relative and become resistant to herbicides.

There is evidence that genetically engineered plants have already spread. The Miracle-Gro Company tested an herbicide-tolerant variety of creeping bent grass, which it planned to sell for use on golf courses. Environmental Protection Agency (EPA) scientists found that six areas near the test site also included the modified grass. Some samples were found more than two miles (3 km) away from the test site. Scientists theorized that wind carried the seeds and pollen of the modified grass to other areas.

Enhanced Breeding Approach

Some critics of genetically modified foods favor using an enhanced breeding approach that would allow crops to be modified without implanting genes from one plant or animal into another.

In traditional breeding, farmers must take a plant with a trait they desire, breed it with another plant that also has desirable traits, and then examine the offspring and hope to find one that has both of the desired traits. Those desired offspring must be crossed to produce a new generation of plants. The process often requires thousands of crosses and can take several years.

Using an enhanced breeding approach, the process can be shortened by years. Many plants do not exhibit desirable characteristics until they are fully grown. In enhanced breeding, researchers would test the genes of a plant early on to determine what traits it has. Scientists would know earlier which plants to cross and which offspring were successful.

Enhanced breeding crosses plants naturally while producing the desired effects. "Classical breeders and geneticists can use the genome but not do gene splicing," explained Jeremy Rifkin, a critic of genetic engineering.[2] He added that a better understanding of genes could also improve organic farming.

Greenpeace petitions the European Union to label milk, meat, and egg products from animals that have been fed genetically modified crops.

There have also been instances where genetically modified crops have unintentionally become part of the food chain. In the summer of 2006, Riceland Foods reported that it had found small amounts of an unapproved herbicide-tolerant rice strain in commercial rice supplies.

That same summer, Greenpeace and Friends of the Earth reported that they discovered traces of an unapproved insect-resistant type of rice in a product that had been imported to London from China. The European Union has urged nations to prevent unapproved genetically engineered foods from entering the food chain.

Opposed: Nature May Adapt to Genetic Modifications

Another concern about food that is resistant to particular pests or herbicides is that nature will adapt to the genetically modified changes. "When we breed traditional plants that are resistant to some particular pest, the next most important pest moves in. We see this all the time with plant viruses," said Allison G. Power, an ecology professor at Cornell University.[3]

In Favor: Genetically Modified Crops Cut Down on the Use of Pesticides

In some ways, genetically modifying food can actually help the environment. Most

Ben & Jerry's against Cloning

Ben & Jerry's Homemade has made a name for itself by producing great flavors of ice cream. But the company is also making a name for itself with its stance against cloning. Jerry Greenfield, one of the founders of the ice cream brand, said that the ice cream maker is planning on putting labels on its ice cream guaranteeing that it is made using products that come from clone-free cows. "Putting cloned animals and their milk in our food supply is just weird, and people don't want it," according to Greenfield.[4]

The Food and Drug Administration currently has no plans to prevent meat and milk from cloned animals from entering the food supply, despite complaints from Greenfield and others.

Monsanto

Monsanto is one of the largest biotechnology firms in the world. It is also one of the most widely criticized companies for its use of genetically modified products.

It provides biotechnology traits for insect protection and herbicide tolerance. It also sells Roundup, a popular herbicide. Monsanto is also the leading provider of genetically modified seeds.

genetically engineered foods are modified to be resistant to pesticides. This cuts down on the use of potentially harmful chemicals, reducing the risk of chemicals from entering the water supply. According to one recent report, 380 million pounds (172 million kg) of pesticides that normally would have been used between 1996 and 2004 were not used as a result of genetically modified crops. Many believe that the use of pesticides will go down even more in the future as genetically modified foods become more popular.

Zigfridas Vaituzis, a senior scientist at the Environmental Protection Agency, thinks genetic modifications are beneficial:

With herbicide-tolerant crops, farmers can spray their fields with relatively safe, biodegradable chemicals. For its part, (genetically modified) cotton has cut pesticide use on cotton crops by half. ... that means less exposure to those chemicals, both on the farm, in ground water and in spray drift in the surrounding community. Those are measurable benefits.[5]

In Favor: Genetically Modified Foods Are Safe

In the United States, genetically modified foods are not regulated much differently than any other type of food. When genetically modified foods were beginning to be mass produced for sale in supermarkets, the FDA tested these foods.

The FDA determined that labeling these foods as genetically modified was unnecessary because there was no evidence of health risks and the nutritional content was the same as the non-modified food. This policy was established in 1992, when the FDA issued a statement that said genetically engineered crops were "'substantially similar' to conventional crops."[6]

Public Opinion

According to a 2005 survey conducted by the Food Policy Institute at Rutgers University, U.S. citizens are confused about issues regarding genetic engineering. That survey of 1,200 residents

found that half of those polled were unsure or could not take a position on genetically modified foods. Approximately 25 percent approved of the technology. However, about the same amount of people disapproved. Perhaps most surprising was that the survey showed fewer than half of the respondents realized that supermarkets sell genetically modified foods on a regular basis.

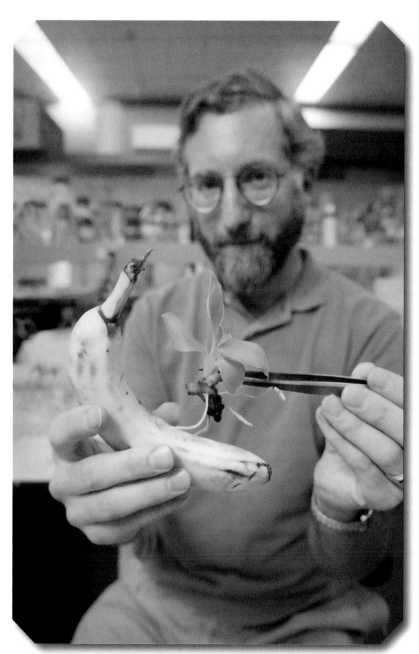

Dr. Neal Gutterson shows a genetically altered banana that ripens more slowly and has a longer shelf life than organic bananas.

A genetically altered mouse that produces human antibodies

CREATING CHIMERAS

One of the goals of scientists working on genetic engineering is to produce new technologies and tools that will help the medical community. For instance, scientists can look for new ways to help people who have a deficiency of a certain protein or antibodies. Scientists look for new ways to cure Parkinson's disease, diabetes, and cancer. Genetic engineering could help scientists answer these problems.

CHIMERAS

Sweetheart looks like a normal goat. She has brown stripes and is calm. But she has been genetically engineered. Her DNA contains a single human gene that allows her to produce a protein in her milk that is normally found in human blood. The milk contains antithrombin, a protein that helps blood clot, which has become a life-saving drug for humans.

Sweetheart, created by GTC Biotherapeutics, is just one example of a modern-day animal-human chimera—an organism that has DNA from a human and one or more additional sources. In Greek

CopyCat

In 2002, researchers in Texas cloned a domestic cat that they named CopyCat (also known as Carbon Copy). CopyCat was a genetic clone of her mother. According to Mark Westhusin, who helped clone the cat, there are serious medical reasons to clone felines. "Cats have a feline AIDS that is a good model for studying human AIDS," he said.[1]

mythology, a chimera is a hybrid beast that breathed fire and appeared before a natural disaster.

GTC has been able to create its transgenic goats with an almost 100 percent success rate. Transgenic organisms contain altered genomes. Pharmaceutical firms and investors went wild when GTC introduced its transgenic goats. The stock eventually fell, but GTC proved that the pharmaceutical industry and the investing public are very enthusiastic about the prospects of using chimeras and genetic engineering for biomedical research.

Another animal-human chimera is a mouse that contains a replica of a human immune system. The mouse can produce human antibodies that can be harvested and inserted into humans to help fight disease.

Fifty biotechnology and pharmaceutical companies have started using mice with human immune systems to produce

Chimeras

Chimeras that scientists have developed include:
• Pigs with human genes that can produce kidneys, hearts, and other organs that are more suitable for use in humans;
• Rabbits whose blood contains human antibodies that may be used to treat human diseases;
• Cows with antibodies in their blood that can be used to treat diseases; and
• Chickens that lay eggs containing human proteins that may one day be used to create useful drugs.

Cloned calves have been genetically engineered to produce human antibodies.

human antibodies. These antibodies may be used to develop treatments for diseases ranging from cancer to lupus.

Goats and mice are not the only transgenic organisms (organisms whose genomes have been altered) that scientists are trying to use to develop treatments for diseases that afflict humans. Researchers are also trying to extract drugs from transgenic chicken eggs.

In Favor: Chimeras Can Help Cure Disease

Many scientists feel that animal testing is an essential step in scientific research. To these scientists, using animals to produce human genes is a similar and important step in scientific discovery. Animal-human chimeras have immense potential to help humans suffering from disease. Harry M. Meade created the mice that produce human antibodies. According to Meade, "their cells produce antibodies in exactly the right form to go into humans."[2] The antibodies can be produced in mass quantities and used to create drugs for humans.

Some researchers say that cells produced by chimeras would be fit for human implantation. They believe the possibilities that chimeras present could cure many diseases.

Opposed: Chimeras Could Make Healthy People Ill

Critics are concerned that animal-human chimeras could leak into the food supply. If a chimera mated with a normal animal, its offspring may still have the human gene. If these animals reached the food supply, there is a concern that healthy people could be made ill. Many groups state that the FDA has not fully restricted chimeras from entering the food supply when research is completed. The animals could also be released from laboratories if animal rights groups were to break in and "liberate" the animals, as they have been known to do.

Critics are also concerned about the moral implications of inserting human genes into animals. Religious opponents might argue that science has gone too far and to insert human genes into

Alzheimer's Gene Turned Off in Mice

Researching genes in animals is essential in determining how similar changes in genetics could affect humans. In May 2007, researchers at the University of Texas Southwestern Medical Center reported that they had turned off a gene associated with Alzheimer's disease in mice, and when they did so, the mice appeared to have become smarter. Researchers reported that the mice were better able to learn how to navigate a water maze and remember the cages in which they received an electric shock.

"We have shown that we can turn off a gene in an adult animal. That has never been done before," said Dr. James Bibb, assistant professor of psychiatry at the medical center.[3] News of the study was published in the *Nature Neuroscience* journal.

However, when scientists tried to breed mice that lacked the gene altogether, the mice died. To survive and exhibit the increased intelligence, the gene had to be kept but turned off.

Researchers at the medical center are still looking at the long-term effects that turning the gene off may have on the mice. The gene that was manipulated controls the production of a brain enzyme that is connected to diseases caused by the loss of neurons, such as Alzheimer's.

animals goes against God. For some, the knowledge that animals can contain human genes means redefining their personal definitions of what it means to be human.

The idea that science should not tinker with human life is a common argument against genetic sciences. This argument is most widely cited in the debate over cloning.

A scientist inserts stem cells containing human genes into a chicken embryo.

Researchers at the Harvard Stem Cell Institute clone stem cells in hopes of treating diseases.

CLONING

lones are organisms that are nearly genetically identical. Clones occur naturally as identical twins or as plants produced by asexual reproduction (self-fertilizing). However, scientists have begun creating clones of bacteria, plants, and animals in laboratories. Cloning in this way is a type of genetic engineering.

There is no proof that scientists have successfully cloned a human. Some scientists do not believe it is possible. Others believe that human cloning could be done the same way in which genetic engineers clone embryos for stem cell research. Instead of destroying the embryo and developing embryonic stem cells, the embryo would be transferred to a woman's uterus and allowed to grow into a baby. The baby would be a human clone.

HUMAN CLONING

With the cloning of Dolly in 1996, people began speculating whether it was possible to clone a human and whether that would be ethical.

Several attempts have been made to clone a human, but there is no evidence to show that any of these attempts have been successful.

The Cloning of a Man

Long before the cloning of Dolly, some people were convinced that a human had been cloned. Freelance science writer David Rorvik wrote *In His Image: The Cloning of a Man*. Published in 1978, the book convinced many people that a billionaire had himself cloned.

According to the book, the billionaire had found a scientist who implanted a cloned embryo into a woman. The woman gave birth to the cloned child in 1976.

The book sparked outrage and led to congressional hearings. At the time, many people said cloning a human was impossible. Eventually, the story was proved to be a hoax.

At least one American company and one American university have attempted to produce cloned human embryos, but they did not transfer them to a woman's uterus. Other attempts to clone a human have been made in China and other parts of the world. Scientists at Stanford University have said they intend to try creating cloned human embryos for research.

Michael J. Fox

One of the most prominent advocates of embryonic stem cell research, which is interwoven with the debate over cloning and genetic engineering, is actor Michael J. Fox. Fox was diagnosed with Parkinson's disease in 1991, but he kept it a secret for seven years. Since disclosing his condition in 1998, he has tirelessly campaigned for using stem cells to find a cure for Parkinson's disease and other illnesses. In 2000, he launched the Michael J. Fox Foundation for Parkinson's Research.

Scientists have taken small steps toward human cloning through embryonic stem cell research. They have cloned human cells for medical use. For example, scientists can grow new cells from embryonic stem cells to replace a damaged pancreas in a diabetic person. There are different methods to create embryonic stem cells, but one involves transferring the nucleus from a human cell into a human egg, which creates an embryo that is a clone of the original cell. That embryo contains embryonic stem cells, which can be manipulated to turn into any kind

Muhammad Ali and Michael J. Fox hope that genetic engineering research will shed light on Parkinson's disease.

of cell, including a pancreas cell, and implanted into the patient. People's immune systems recognize foreign cells and attack these cells. Scientists hope that by creating cells this way, as clones of the original, the body will accept the implanted cells more readily.

Doctors' Decision

Despite the potential benefits of cloning and embryonic stem cell research, doctors and scientists

Cloning Neanderthals?

According to researchers at the Max Planck Institute for Evolutionary Anthropology in Leipzig, Germany, it would be possible to reconstruct the genome of a Neanderthal. Cloning Neanderthals could help resolve an age-old question: Are Neanderthals related to modern humans? Some people believe that Neanderthals and modern humans interbred while others argue that humans simply replaced Neanderthals.

Other scientists doubt that the genome of a Neanderthal could be completely reconstructed due to contamination and decay of the DNA.

must make a moral decision about whether they will participate in this research. Doctors are in a difficult position. According to the American Medical Association (AMA) Web site,

While the ... moral visions that underlie this debate must be respected, physicians collectively must continue to be guided by their paramount obligation to the welfare of their patients. ... [A] physician remains free to decide whether to participate in stem cell research or to use its products.[1]

The AMA urges the following for embryonic stem cell research:

❖ Biomedical research requires appropriate oversight and monitoring.

❖ Subjects must agree to participate in biomedical research if any embryos they are donating are to be destroyed.

❖ Participants must be informed that in order to

extract stem cells from an embryo, the embryo will need to be destroyed.

❖ Subjects must understand the uses of the research.

OPPOSED: CLONING RAISES ETHICAL CONCERNS

Although Congress has yet to pass a bill to ban human reproductive cloning in the United States, the President's Council on Bioethics is against the idea of human cloning. Since the idea of human cloning has reached the forefront of public awareness, the Council has conducted a review

Cloning Hits Hollywood

Just as cloning has fascinated scientists, it has also caught the attention of those in Hollywood. Moviemakers have produced movies about human cloning for decades. These movies include:

- *Invasion of the Body Snatchers*, made in 1956, tells the story of residents of a small town who are cloned when strange pods are placed beside them as they sleep. Their clones try to take over the world.
- *Blade Runner*, made in 1982, features clones that have traveled to Earth in an attempt to take over the planet.
- *Terminator 2*, made in 1991, features a futuristic clone that travels in time to try to save a human who will help save the world.
- *Multiplicity* made in 1996, tells the story of an overworked man who tries to solve his problems by cloning himself and then putting his clones to work.

of the legal and ethical issues raised by the prospect
of cloning humans.

On its Web site, the council states that cloning to
produce children,

> *... raises deep concerns about identity and individuality,
> the meaning of having children, the difference between
> procreation and manufacture, and the relationship between
> the generations.* [2]

Opposed: Cloning Violates Religious Beliefs

Many people say that cloning violates religious
principles or is unnatural. Cardinal William Keeler,
archbishop of Baltimore, believes that cloning
violates sanctity and dignity of human life. Keeler
wrote,

> *We believe a society can be judged by the respect it shows
> for human life, especially in its most vulnerable stages and
> conditions. On this basis the Catholic Church strongly opposes
> the taking of human life through abortion, euthanasia or
> destructive experiments on human embryos.* [3]

Opposed: Cloning Is Dangerous

A common problem with the cloning of animals
is a condition known as large offspring syndrome.

An animal implanted with a cloned embryo often has a longer pregnancy. This can result in a difficult pregnancy and birth. The offspring is heavier than normal and sometimes has difficulty breathing after birth and dies. Other times, the offspring will develop abnormal kidneys or other organs.

Scientists theorize that advanced reproductive technologies, such as genetic engineering, can disturb the way that genetic instructions are carried out. Most of the time, large offspring syndrome does not result in problems that are fatal and a clone does not pass the condition to its offspring.

Do We Need Human Egg Cells to Clone Humans?

Scientists have a difficult time acquiring human eggs for research. It is a time consuming and painful process, and many women are not willing to donate. People have been trying for years to clone human cells without using an egg from a woman. Three teams of British scientists are researching this possibility. These scientists feel that cloning is hindered because there is a shortage of human egg cells.

"Getting eggs from women is the bottleneck to cloning, an alternative would be welcome," according to Jose Cibelli.[4]

In Favor: Cloning a Loved One

Some advocates of human cloning want to clone human children who would be virtually identical to preexisting individuals. Scientists believe human cloning would allow infertile couples to

Cloned piglets

have children who are genetically related to them. Moreover, it may also allow couples that are at risk of having a child with a genetic disease to be assured that their children will be healthy.

There are other potential uses as well. For instance, scientists could clone someone who had exceptional abilities. Or they may seek to clone a person who was about to die. There is much debate over whether it would be beneficial or moral for parents who are about to lose a child to clone their loved one.

In Favor: Cloning Is Similar to In-vitro Fertilization

Nathan Myhrvold, a quantum physicist and the former chief technical officer at Microsoft, does not see any issue with cloning humans. Myhrvold and others who support human cloning do not see the process as being much different from in-vitro fertilization, a process in which the egg is fertilized outside the uterus and implanted later. They do not think that the genetic identity of a person is morally significant. In an essay on human cloning, Myhrvold wrote,

> The cloning procedure is similar to in vitro fertilization. The only difference is that the DNA of sperm and egg would be replaced by DNA from an adult cell. What law or principle— secular, humanist or religious—says that one combination of genetic material in a flask is OK, but another is not?[5]

Myhrvold believes that fear of clones is just another form of racism. He believes that people should have the option to have a cloned child in cases where one parent carries a gene that could result in a genetic disease or when couples are infertile.

In Favor: Religion Should Not Play a Role

Many people are opposed to cloning on religious and moral grounds. Those who support cloning do not feel that religion should play a role in scientific discovery. They feel that religion should apply to an individual's actions and decisions but not apply to others who do not hold the same beliefs. The head of the Catholic Church, Pope Benedict XVI, has expressed his opposition to human cloning. In an essay supporting cloning, Myhrvold wrote:

> ... calling for secular governments to implement a ban, thus extending [the pope's] power beyond those he can persuade, shows rather explicitly that the pope does not respect the freedom of others.[6]

While Myhrvold respects the pope and the views of other religious groups, he argues that the views of religious opponents are outdated and should be reevaluated in light of today's science. ⌒

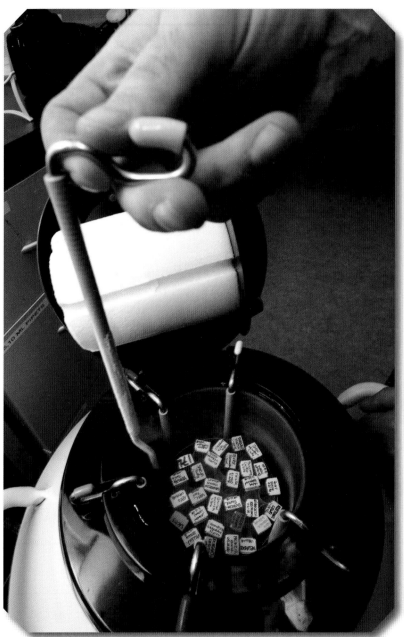

Eggs donated for stem cell research

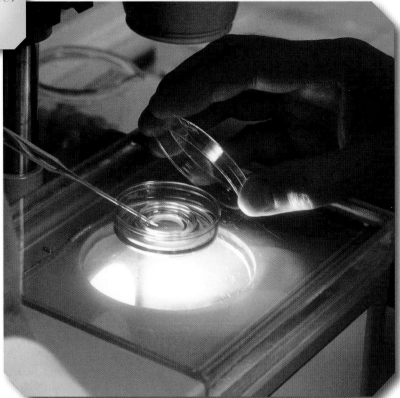

Embryos prepared for in-vitro fertilization can be tested for diseases.

Eugenics

ugenics is a science that seeks to manipulate genes to create a superior breed of human. The idea of eugenics was born in 1833. Sir Francis Galton came up with a theory that said that if intelligent, talented people married each other and had children, the result would be unusually talented children.

Some argue that there is nothing wrong with the idea of manipulating genes so that children have more desirable traits. They believe that it would be acceptable to modify genes to make a child more intelligent, talented, or beautiful (if this were possible).

Opposed: Eugenics Promotes Racism

The idea of eugenics spread. Some governments forced eugenics on its people to promote racist philosophies and create a superior race. People such as Adolf Hitler have used the idea to defend their racist actions. During World War II, Hitler tried to exterminate the Jewish population and create a superior race. The idea of certain races being better than others still exists. Wars are waged in which the ultimate goal is the elimination of another race.

Eugenics has been used to support sterilization programs, such as one in North Carolina from 1929 to 1974. Although the women were not forcibly sterilized, they were strongly encouraged to consent to do so. Poor women or women of a certain race were urged to be sterilized or to have abortions. The reason for this program was to help society and prevent unwanted children. However, many consider programs such as these to be unethical.

One Man's Crusade to Help Victims of Eugenics

In North Carolina, a program in place from 1929 to 1974 led to more than 7,600 people to be talked into being sterilized for reasons such as "feeble-mindedness." Even though most other states stopped sterilization programs based on eugenics in the 1960s, North Carolina continued to implement its program.

Representative Larry Womble of Winston-Salem, North Carolina, has been trying to help those who were sterilized against their will in North Carolina. For four years, Womble has been working to introduce legislation to aid these people.

Womble wants those who were sterilized to be given $50,000 each in reparations. Funding concerns have prevented Womble's bill from being passed. However, state officials have agreed to provide some sort of compensation to the victims. In 2003, North Carolina Governor Mike Easley issued an apology for the sterilization program. He also approved recommendations that the victims of the sterilization program be compensated with education and health care benefits.

OPPOSED: DESIGNER BABIES WOULD INCREASE COMPETITION

Countries such as Canada, South Africa, and Australia have banned the practice of creating "designer babies." Designer babies are babies whose genes have been altered to make them more desirable. Not all countries have banned the practice; the United States continues to allow the practice. Manipulating genes to create a more desirable human being is an example of how the idea of eugenics is evolving in light of new science.

Eric G. Swedin, of Weber State University, foresees China becoming interested in eugenics and speculates that creating a superior race could become a competition between nations. While the Soviet Union and United States once competed with each other over sending the first person to space, Swedin suggests there could be a day when two countries compete to create a superior person. In a 2006 article that appeared in *The Futurist*, Swedin wrote:

> *A future of human eugenics is not something to take lightly. … Around the world, parents seeking the best opportunities for their children may want to buy biotechnology that gives their children an edge, and we will see the birth of specialized human beings. Moral qualms will be brushed aside, and keeping up with the Chinese will be seen as a patriotic duty.*[1]

Opposed: Governments Oppose Modifying Embryos

As of July 2006, 21 countries had signed and ratified an agreement at a Council of Europe convention. Thirteen others have signed the agreement but have not ratified it. The agreement bans tampering with a human embryo in order to create changes that can be passed from generation to generation.

While the United States has not banned making genetic modifications to human embryos that could be passed on to other generations, many other countries have. The FDA's stance on the issue is that embryos should not be so modified.

OPPOSED: UNFORESEEN RESULTS

Some eugenics opponents argue that even if genetic diseases could be prevented, it may not always be beneficial for society as a whole. For instance, manic depression, an illness that causes a person to experience elevated and depressive states lasting from three to six months, can cause an individual to suffer. However, many of the world's most creative thinkers suffered from the condition or some other genetic disorder. It is possible that curing people of these illnesses would deprive the world of great artists, musicians, and thinkers.

There could also be unforeseen consequences to altering people's genes too much. Lee Silver, a biologist at Princeton University, believes genetic modifications could get out of scientists' control. In his book, *Remaking Eden*, Silver suggests that centuries of genetic engineering could lead to the creation of a new species of human that would be incapable of mating with its "gene-poor" relations.

Other scientists also fear the unintended consequences of eugenics. According to Liebe Cavalieri, a molecular biologist at the State University of New York, "The potential power of genetic engineering is far greater than that of splitting the atom, and it could be every bit as dangerous to society."[2]

In Favor: Eugenics Helps Prevent the Spread of Genetic Diseases

As far as genetic engineering is concerned, eugenics usually involves the manipulation of embryos in a dish rather than the extermination of people. Dr. Mark

Woo Suk Hwang

In 2004 and 2005, Woo Suk Hwang shocked the world when he claimed to have cloned human embryos and derived embryonic stem cells from those cloned embryos. In January 2006, a university panel determined that Hwang had fabricated his results.

The scandal led the scientific community to question other findings. Hwang was later charged with fraud, bioethics violations, and embezzling millions of dollars. He could face up to ten years in prison if he is convicted of all charges. Five members of his research team also have been charged for their roles in the fraud.

Hughes developed a way to test embryos for genetic diseases in the 1990s. Hughes wanted to diagnose a genetic disease before a couple became pregnant. He wanted to ease the suffering of couples by uncovering genetic disorders.

In this test, the couple must undergo in-vitro fertilization, which is a process that involves fertilizing an egg and sperm in a laboratory dish. After the egg is fertilized, scientists extract a cell from each of the fertilized embryos. The embryos can then be tested for genetic diseases. This procedure is usually done for couples who have a genetic disease that runs in their family, such as cystic fibrosis. The couple can then choose to implant an embryo that is free of any disease. If this practice becomes widespread, genetic disorders could one day be eliminated.

In Favor: Public Support

Evidence shows that many members of the public do not have serious problems with the idea of genetically altering their children to ensure that they do not develop genetic problems. Polls have shown that up to 20 percent of people support altering genes to make their children genetically superior.

Some suggest that a couple could test embryos for more than genetic diseases. They could select only to implant embryos that had certain desirable traits—such as gender, height, or a particular body type.

Designing babies is already occurring on a small scale. For instance, Dr. Abayomi Ajayi of the Nordical Fertility Clinic in Lagos, Nigeria, said embryos there are being screened for particular characteristics such as sex. They also use screening to determine whether the embryo will develop a genetic disease, such as sickle-cell anemia.

In Favor: New Cures for Diseases

Some scientists believe it is their duty to use genetic engineering to try to cure genetic diseases before they occur. One day, it may be possible for a scientist to cure a genetic disease in someone by modifying a human embryo. Robert Taylor wrote an article for *New Scientist* that offers an example:

> Suppose, for instance, that men in your family tend to get prostate cancer at a young age. Insert into your fertilized egg [a human artificial chromosome] containing a gene for a toxin that kills any cell that makes it, and two switches for that gene—one that is turned on only by prostate cells and another

Indiana Apologizes for Eugenics

In 1907, Indiana Governor J. Frank Hanly signed into law what is believed to be the first U.S. bill that permitted sterilization in an effort to try to limit the gene pool. From 1907 to 1974, Indiana sterilized approximately 25,000 people. A total of 65,000 people were sterilized in the United States during this period. Although many of these people were not forcibly sterilized, they were encouraged to do so.

In April 2007, the state apologized for its role in sterilizing people. Many people believe that other states should do the same. Many of the same questions that surrounded the eugenics of earlier times still apply today when looked at in tandem with genetic engineering.

by ecdysonen, an insect hormone that humans cannot make. Nine months later, you're delivered of a bouncing baby boy. Fifty years later, he gets prostate cancer. He takes ecdysonen, which activates the prostate poison, killing every prostate cell in his body. Even cancer cells that have spread to other parts of the body should be wiped out.[3]

The potential of such procedures—called germ-line engineering—excites scientists. Leroy Hood, a molecular biologist at the University of Washington in Seattle, said, "We could probably engineer people to be totally resistant to AIDS, or to certain kinds of cancers. We might engineer people to live much longer. I would say all these are good qualities."[4]

Oregon Governor John Kitzhaber signs an apology for the state's past use of forced sterilization.

President George W. Bush is opposed to using healthy human embryos
for research.

POLITICS

The arguments for and against genetic
engineering have led to a great deal of
debate in the United States, in the European
Union, and across the globe. In the United States,
117 pieces of legislation were related to agricultural
biotechnology in 2005. This legislation covered

33 states and the District of Columbia. Twenty-three bills related to genetic engineering were passed in 2005. Two-thirds of these bills supported technology tied to genetic engineering, according to the Pew Initiative on Food and Biotechnology.

PATENTS

Most people are familiar with the notion of getting a patent for an invention. But companies now are seeking and receiving patents on genes, which has led to a great deal of controversy. Gene patents are for specific sequences of DNA and how they can be used.

Some people dislike the idea of patenting genes because they feel that it limits scientific research. Also, there are few regulations on what exactly can and cannot be patented. Those looking to make scientific advancements in genetics feel that patents slow progress and increase costs. This not only limits research, but limits options for

Senator John Charles Kunich: Cloning Should Be Allowed

Senator John Charles Kunich of California, as well as many other legislators, believes that opponents of cloning need to reevaluate their views. Kunich told *Popular Science,* "You're going to lose out on a whole lot of medical treatments that might otherwise be available to you, or your spouse or someone you love. Beyond that, it's really hard to draw lines between reproductive cloning and other things like in vitro fertilization that people have grown quite fond of. And if government can ban a whole category of research because they don't like the subject matter, that opens the door for other types of censorship."[1]

medical testing for disease because many patients cannot afford tests that require a payment be made to the patent owner.

In addition to patenting genes, genetically modified organisms can be patented. This idea took hold in 1980 as a result of a Supreme Court decision. Ananda Mohan Chakrabarty, an employee at General Electric, sought a patent for an oil-eating bacterium. The court ruled that life created in a laboratory could indeed be patented.

In 1988, the U.S. Patent Office granted a patent on a transgenic mouse. Researchers at Harvard University had engineered a

Would a Ban on Cloning Harm the United States?

The issue of whether or not to ban all human cloning (to create embryos for cloning and to create cloned children) has been hotly debated for years. So far, no real resolution has been agreed upon. In the United States, opponents of a complete ban argue that it would simply move research overseas. If this happened, the United States would begin to fall behind other nations in scientific knowledge and advancement. Carl B. Feldbaum, president of the Biotechnology Industry Organization, a trade group, told a congressional committee in 2002, "Criminalizing therapeutic cloning and treatments based on the technology ... would move the research and its benefits overseas and out of reach of Americans."[2]

But organizations including the National Right to Life Committee, the United Methodist Church General Board, Friends of the Earth, and others believe that a complete human cloning ban is necessary to protect the sanctity of human life.

mouse that was susceptible to breast cancer. They had created the mouse so they could test medicine and vaccines on the mice before testing them on humans. Although patents such as these allow companies to make money from their research, many do not feel that living organisms should fall under patent law.

OPPOSED: PATENTING HUMAN GENES PREVENTS FURTHER RESEARCH

Approximately 20 percent of the human genome is already patented. The patenting of human genes has led politicians, such as Florida Representative Dave Weldon, to express their concern about whether researchers and companies "own" human DNA or the genetic heritage of the human race.

In 2007, Weldon cosponsored a bill that would forbid further patenting of human genetic material. In an interview with *Florida Today*, Weldon expressed his concern:

> *Gene patenting is interfering with patient access to treatments and the free flow of scientific information. If I patent the gene for macular degeneration (a cause of blindness), I can say you cannot work on this gene, unless you pay me. It's outrageous.*[3]

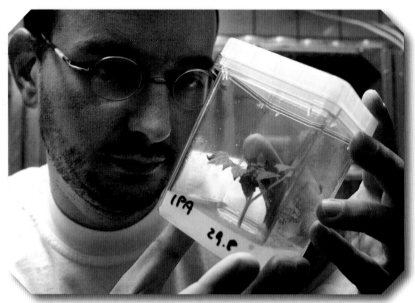

Biologist Ralph Bock has a patent on this genetically engineered tomato plant.

In Favor: Patents Protect Research

Patents are designed to protect scientists' inventions. Because genetic modifications are not natural developments, they are allowed patents. This prevents others from using the inventor's idea without permission.

Some politicians and scientists argue that the most important genes already have patents taken out on them, so it really would not hurt businesses much to stop the practice now before it gets out of hand. These patents expire 20 years after they are issued. Then, anyone can work on the genes. Some politicians feel it is best to allow the patents to expire rather than make changes to patent law. Congress continues to debate patent issues that involve the human genome.

Recent Developments in the United States

Whether or not to expand federal funding for embryonic stem cell research has ignited a fury of controversy in the United States. In 2006, President George W. Bush vetoed legislation to expand federal backing of projects using embryonic stem cells. The Bush administration has limited the embryonic stem cell lines that can be used for research to embryos that have already been destroyed. President Bush feels that it is immoral to destroy an embryo that has the potential to develop into a human being.

Expanding federal funding for embryonic stem cell research would help researchers make progress. Members of Congress have said they intend to pass another measure that would allow more federal funding for embryonic stem cell research, but the president has stated that he plans to veto the measure.

IN FAVOR: STEM CELL RESEARCH SHOULD BE EXPLORED

Supporters of stem cell research say that knowledge gathered through stem cell research could be applied to treat Parkinson's disease, Alzheimer's disease, and other ailments that have devastating consequences. As of 2007, there were federal funding limits on such research.

According to Utah Senator Orin Hatch, "The help offered by stem cell research is too great to ignore." The Republican Senator believes that Bush is on "the wrong side of history."[4]

EUROPE'S STANCE ON GENETICALLY MODIFIED FOODS

While the U.S. FDA does not strictly regulate genetically modified food, Europe has not followed that example. As

Christopher Reeve

Christopher Reeve was an actor best known for his role as Superman. He became a tireless advocate for embryonic stem cell research after he was paralyzed as a result of a horseback riding accident in 1995.

The actor began promoting research on the beneficial potential of experimenting on stem cells. He had a profound effect on the nation's awareness of stem cell research.

Reeve pushed President George W. Bush to allow federal funding on embryonic stem cells in 2001. He was hopeful that stem cell research could one day benefit victims of paralysis. Although Reeve never significantly recovered from his accident, his courage inspired many. Reeve died October 10, 2004, at the age of 52.

genetically modified foods became prevalent in the 1990s, farmers, environmentalists, and consumer organizations throughout Europe staged protests to voice their concerns about selling such food to consumers.

The European Union initiated a detailed review process for genetically modified food. Genetically modified food was separated from the regular food supply and tracked. The modified food was labeled and tested. However, stores in Europe do not typically supply genetically modified foods. Many consumers in Europe are wary of eating such foods.

A Complicated Issue

Genetic engineering poses many questions that scientists, legislators, doctors, and consumers all have to answer. While some believe that genetic engineering has the

Senator Sam Brownback

Kansas Senator Sam Brownback has gained support from the pro-life community for his stance against embryonic stem cell research. Brownback believes that life begins at conception and should be protected. "I'm not willing to say, 'Well, we can research on you when you're 10 days old and not 10 years old,'" the senator said at a speech at Georgetown University.[5]

Brownback believes that embryonic stem cell research is not necessary because scientists can conduct experiments on adult stem cells. "I want to find a cure ... and I believe we have a way of doing it without sacrificing the sacredness of humans," he said.[6]

potential to do much good, others believe it also has the potential to do immense harm.

Both sides of the issue must be looked at. The potential benefit of genetic engineering and cloning may justify researching these areas further. However, the potential risks weigh just as heavily on the decision. ⌐

Biologist Elizabeth Blackburn was appointed to the President's Council on Bioethics in 2001.

Timeline

8000 BCE	1627	1859
Humans domesticate crops and livestock. They begin breeding animals.	Francis Bacon predicts the future use of genetic engineering.	Charles Darwin publishes *The Origin of Species*, which details information about breeding, natural selection, and evolution.

1953	1961	1972
James Watson and Francis Crick propose that DNA is a double-helix structure.	Sidney Brenner, François Jacob, and Matthew Meselson discover messenger RNA.	Using an in-vitro fertilization process, Paul Berg makes recombinant DNA.

1863	1910	1944
While experimenting with pea plants, Gregor Mendel discovers that traits are inherited through predictable patterns.	T.H. Morgan proves that chromosomes carry genes, which include the information responsible for genetic traits.	Oswald Avery shows that DNA carries genetic information, not RNA or protein.

1973	1978	1979
Herbert Boyer and Stanley Cohen perform the first recombinant DNA cloning experiment.	On July 25, Louise Brown is born as a result of in-vitro fertilization.	Insulin is produced through genetic engineering.

TIMELINE

1983	1986	1987
The gene that contains human growth hormone is placed into a mouse embryo, producing a mouse twice the normal size.	Embryo cells from a sheep are cloned.	Mice with human genes are created. A plant that is resistant to an herbicide is created.

1992	1997	2000
The FDA rules that genetically engineered foods are "not inherently dangerous" and do not need special regulation.	Scientists at the Roslin Institute in Scotland clone a sheep using a mammary cell from an adult sheep.	On October 2, the first genetically modified primate is born.

1990	1991	1992
James Watson and others begin the Human Genome Project to map the entire human genome.	Gene therapy trials on humans begin.	Calgene's Flavr-Savr tomato is approved for commercial production.

2001	2001	2005
Parliament agrees to allow scientists to clone human embryos for research purposes in England.	On February 11, the first draft of the human genome is published in *Nature and Science*.	The amount of farmland used to grow genetically altered crops is estimated at 222 million acres.

ESSENTIAL FACTS

AT ISSUE

Opposed

❖ Genetic engineering goes against some religious teachings.

❖ Genetic modifications could lead to the end of sexual reproduction.

❖ There could be mistakes in the cloning process that hurt the clone.

❖ Science could become solely a commercial enterprise that benefits large corporations.

❖ Eugenics could be used to create a master race or to wage violence.

In Favor

❖ Genetic engineering could help infertile couples have children.

❖ Closer organ matches for those in need of transplants could be provided through genetic engineering.

❖ Cloning could help ease the suffering of a person who has lost a loved one.

❖ Crops that are resistant to pests can be grown without the use of pesticides.

❖ Genetic engineering could advance science in ways that currently cannot be understood.

CRITICAL DATES

1859
Charles Darwin published *On the Origin of Species by Means of Natural Selection*, which detailed his theories on evolution and natural selection.

1863
While experimenting with pea plants, Gregor Mendel discovered that traits are inherited through predictable patterns.

1953
Francis Crick and James Watson published their findings regarding the double-helix structure of deoxyribonucleic acid.

1990
The Human Genome Project began.

1997
Ian Wilmut and his associates at the Roslin Institute in Scotland cloned a sheep using a mammary cell from an adult sheep. The birth of Dolly shocked the world and led to debate about cloning.

February 11, 2001
The first draft of the human genome—estimated to be between 26,000 and 40,000 genes—was published in *Nature and Science*.

Quotes

"The prospect of cloning-to-produce children, which would be a radically new form of procreation, raises deep concerns about identity and individuality, the meaning of having children, the difference between procreation and manufacture, and the relationship between the generations." —*The President's Council for Bioethics*

"You're going to lose out on a whole lot of medical treatments that might otherwise be available to you, or your spouse or someone you love. Beyond that, it's really hard to draw lines between reproductive cloning and other things like in vitro fertilization that people have grown quite fond of. And if government can ban a whole category of research because they don't like the subject matter, that opens the door for other types of censorship." —*Senator John Charles Kunich*

ADDITIONAL RESOURCES

SELECT BIBLIOGRAPHY

Brown, Kathryn. "Seeds of Concern." *Scientific American*. 16. 4. (2006).

Coghlan, Andy. "Genetically Modified Crops: A Decade of Disagreement." *New Scientist*, 189. 2535 (2006).

Reiss, Michael J., and Roger Straughan. *Improving Nature? The Science and Ethics of Genetic Engineering*. Cambridge University Press, 1996.

Swedin, Eric G. "Designing Babies: A Eugenics Race with China?" *The Futurist*. May–June 2006.

Torr, James D., ed. *Medical Ethics*. San Diego: Greenhaven Press, 2000.

FURTHER READING

Allman, Toney. *Stem Cells*. Farmington Hills, MI.: Lucent Books, 2006.

Avise, John C. *The Hope, Hype, and Reality of Genetic Engineering: Remarkable Stories from Agriculture, Industry, Medicine, and the Environment*. New York: Oxford University Press, 2004.

Levine, Harry, and Mildred Vasan, eds. *Genetic Engineering*. Santa Barbara, CA.: ABC-CLIO, 2006.

Nicholi, Desmond S.T. *An Introduction to Genetic Engineering*. Cambridge University Press, 2002.

Torr, James D., ed. *Genetic Engineering*. Detroit, MI: Greenhaven Press, 2006.

Web Links

To learn more about genetic engineering, visit ABDO Publishing Company on the World Wide Web at **www.abdopublishing.com**. Web sites about genetic engineering are featured on our Book Links page. These links are routinely monitored and updated to provide the most current information available.

For More Information

For more information on this subject, contact or visit the following organizations.

Food and Drug Administration
5600 Fishers Lane, Rockville, MD 20857
888-463-6332
www.fda.gov
The federal administration is responsible for determining the safety of genetically modified foods for human consumption.

Greenpeace
702 H Street Northwest, Washington, DC 20001
202-462-1177
www.greenpeace.org/usa
Greenpeace is a volunteer organization committed to protecting the environment. It opposes genetic engineering in plants and animals.

President's Council on Bioethics
1425 New York Avenue Northwest Suite C, Washington, DC 20005
202-296-4669
www.bioethics.gov
Presidential council that researches and advises on the scientific and ethical issues regarding topics such as genetic engineering and cloning.

GLOSSARY

bacteria
> Single-celled organisms that usually are round, spiral, or rod shaped.

bases
> The four chemical compounds that make up the rungs of the double-helix ladder of DNA. A pair of bases makes up each rung, and most genes consist of thousands of base pairs.

biotechnology
> The use of living organisms or other biological systems in the manufacture of products or for environmental management.

chromosome
> A rod-shaped structure in the nucleus of a cell that carries genes. DNA is located in chromosomes.

clone
> A group of genetically identical cells.

DNA
> Deoxyribonucleic acid, commonly referred to as DNA, stores information that determines the hereditary properties of organisms.

dominant gene
> A gene that causes a particular trait to occur in offspring.

embryo
> The developing human from the time of implantation to the end of the eighth week after conception.

enzyme
> A protein that the body produces in order to speed up a chemical reaction.

eugenics
> The science of controlling the human population through breeding or genetic modifications.

gene
> A unit of heredity that is located in a chromosome and that determines specific hereditary traits.

gene splicing
> A technique that allows scientists to alter the genetic makeup of DNA by taking a fragment of DNA from one organism and inserting it into a DNA molecule from another organism, or in some cases, the same organism.

genome
> All the DNA contained in an organism or a cell.

inherited
> A trait that is passed from parents to offspring.

nucleotide
> A subunit of DNA or RNA consisting of a nitrogenous base, a phosphate molecule, and a sugar molecule.

plasmid
> Small, free-floating rings of DNA found in bacteria.

recessive trait
> A trait in an organism that is not present unless the recessive gene from both parents is inherited.

RNA
> Ribonucleic acid. A chemical similar to a single strand of DNA. RNA delivers DNA's genetic message to a cell, where proteins are made.

stem cell
> An unspecialized cell that eventually becomes a specialized cell.

vector
> A genetically modified organism, often a virus, used to insert DNA into a target organism's DNA.

Source Notes

Chapter 1. Genetic Engineering: Its Highs and Lows
None.

Chapter 2. What Is Genetic Engineering?
None.

Chapter 3. Arguments for Genetic Engineering
1. Andy Coghlan. "Genetically Modified Crops: A Decade of Disagreement." *New Scientist*. 189. (2006): 2535.

Chapter 4. Arguments against Genetic Engineering
1. "Of Mice and Germ Warfare." *New York Times*. 28 Jan. 2001.
2. "Jeremy Rifkin: Fears of a Brave New World." *Unesco Courier*. 51. 9. (1998).
3. Genetic Engineering Network: <www.geneticsaction.org.uk>.
4. "Jeremy Rifkin: Fears of a Brave New World." *Unesco Courier*. 51. 9. (1998).
5. Ibid.
6. Ronald Bailey. "A Tale of Two Scientific Consensuses," *Reason Online*. 6 Apr. 2007.

Chapter 5. Genetically Modified Food

1. "Does the World Need GM Foods? Yes." *Scientific American*. 16. 4. (2006).

2. Andrew Pollack. "Gene Research Finds New use in Agricultural Breeding." *New York Times*. 1 Mar. 2001.

3. Kathryn Brown. "Seeds of Concern." *Scientific American*. 16. 4. (2006).

4. Pallavi Gogoi. "The Case Against Cloning" *Businessweek.com*. 7 Mar. 2007. 2 Oct. 2007 <http://www.businessweek.com/bwdaily/dnflash/content/mar2007/db20070306_592550.htm>.

5. Kathryn Brown. "Seeds of Concern." *Scientific American*. 16. 4. (2006).

6. "Does the World Need GM Foods? No." *Scientific American*. 16. 4.

Chapter 6. Creating Chimeras

1. "First pet clone is a cat." BBC News. 15 Feb. 2002.

2. Arlene Weintraub. "Crossing the Gene Barrier." *Business Week*. 3967. (2006).

3. "Turning off Gene Makes Mice Smarter." *Reuters*. 28 May 2007 <http://www.chinadaily.com.cn/world/2007-05/content_88195.htm>.

Source Notes Continued

Chapter 7. Cloning
1. American Medical Association. "Cloning for biomedical research." <http://ama.assn.org/ama/pub/category/11964.html>.
2. The President's Council on Bioethics. <www.bioethics.gov/topics/cloning_faq.html>.
3. James D. Torr, ed. *Medical Ethics.* San Diego, CA: Greenhaven Press, 2000. 153–155.
4. Paul Elias. "Thinking outside the Egg, Scientists Propose Interspecies Cloning." *Grand Haven Tribune.* 25 Mar. 2007.
5. Roman Espejo, ed. *Biomedical Ethics—Opposing Viewpoints.* San Diego, CA: Greenhaven Press, 2003. 18–19.
6. Ibid. 22.

Chapter 8. Eugenics
1. Eric G. Sweedin. Designing Babies: A Eugenics Race with China?" *The Futurist.* 1 May 2006.
2. Robert Taylor. "Superhumans: Like it or not, in a few short years we'll have the power to control our own evolution." *New Scientist.* 160. (1998).
3. Ibid.
4. Ibid.

Chapter 9. Politics

1. Down Strover. "What You're Not Being Told About Cloning." *Popular Science*. 6. 263. (2003).
2. "Emotionally Charged Cloning Debate Pits Advocates of Total Human Ban Against Backers of Biomedical Research." *CQ Weekly*. 60. 14. (2002).
3. Susan Jenks. "Debate grows over patenting of genes." *Florida Today*. 10 Mar. 2007.
4. Thomas Burr. "Hatch: Stem Cell Fight Should be Pressed On." *The Salt Lake Tribune*. 9 Apr. 2007.
5. "Sam Brownback Decries Embryonic Stem cell Research in Georgetown Speech," 19. Mar. 2006 <www.lifenews.com>.
6. Ibid.

INDEX

ABOUT THE AUTHOR

Thomas Parmalee is the author of *Broken Teeth: A Book of Short Stories* and associate editor at Kates-Boylston Publications, a magazine publisher. He has also taught high school history and worked at the *Times of Trenton*, *Bloomberg News*, and the *Asbury Park Press*.

PHOTO CREDITS

CC Studio/Photo Researchers, Inc., cover, 3, 99; Paul Clements/ AP Images, 6, 98 (bottom); Patricia McDonnell/AP Images, 11; Paul Sakuma/AP Images, 17, 95; Alfred Pasieka/Photo Researchers, Inc., 18, 96 (bottom); Sheila Terry/Photo Researchers, Inc., 25; Powell Tribune, Tessa Schweigert/AP Images, 27, 96 (top); Hank Morgan/Photo Researchers, Inc., 28; Phanie/Photo Researchers, Inc., 33; Chris Knapton/Photo Researchers, Inc., 35; Tom Gannam/AP Images, 36; Joe Cavaretta/AP Images, 41; Bob Galbraith/AP Images, 43; Greg Wahl-Stephens/AP Images, 44; Sal Veder/AP Images, 46; Virginia Mayo/AP Images, 50; Court Mast/AP Images, 55; Eric Risberg/AP Images, 56, 98 (top); Dave Weaver/AP Images, 59; Julie Jacobson/AP Images, 63; Chitose Suzuki/AP Images, 64; Kenneth Lambert/AP Images, 67; PPL Therapeutics/AP Images, 72; Sandy Huffaker/Getty Images, 75, 97; Yvonne Hemsey/Getty Images, 76; Don Ryan/AP Images, 85; Gerald Herbert/AP Images, 86; Rothermel/AP Images, 90